Dedicated to my very own cheeky little ships, Erin and Elliot.

They are the light of my life.

A Little Ship Town

Down by the coast, where seagulls play,
There stood a little ship town by the bay.
Fishermen sang, nets swung wide—
Boats bobbed proudly at every tide.

Then one wild storm came roaring through,
It crashed and it thundered the whole night too.
When daylight came, the docks were grey—
The ships lay wrecked across the bay.

Only two small boats were left that morn:
Young Erin and Elliot, brave though worn.
They watched the townsfolk, tired and sad,
Counting the ships they once had.

The fishermen sighed, "Our fleet is gone!
No ships to fish, no work, no song."
Erin looked out at the empty sea,
And whispered, "If not us… then who will it be?"

"We're just two little ships," said Erin, small,
"But maybe two ships can help them all."
Elliot frowned, "I'm scared… we'll sink!"
But Erin said, "Be brave… just think!"

"I've got it!" she shouted, "We'll build anew—
We'll fix the old ships, that's what we'll do!"
So off they sailed to Boggy Bay,
Where Big Bertie the Smelly-Ship liked to stay.

Bertie was grumpy, his decks full of goo,
His bilge smelled worse than old sea stew.
"Oh ship," he groaned, "What do you two need?"
"We need your help so the town can feed!"

Bertie sighed, then puffed a plume,
"Well… my bay's been lonely, full of gloom.
If we get our ships together, quick,
We'll rebuild that fleet in just a tick."

They searched the shallows, splashing and diving,
Where pieces of ship from the wrecks were surviving.
Broken planks, bent masts, tangled rope—
Each bit they found gave them new hope.

They hauled the timber, dried each plank,
Stacked them neatly along the bank.
With Bertie's tools and Elliot's grip,
They built the bones of a brand-new ship.

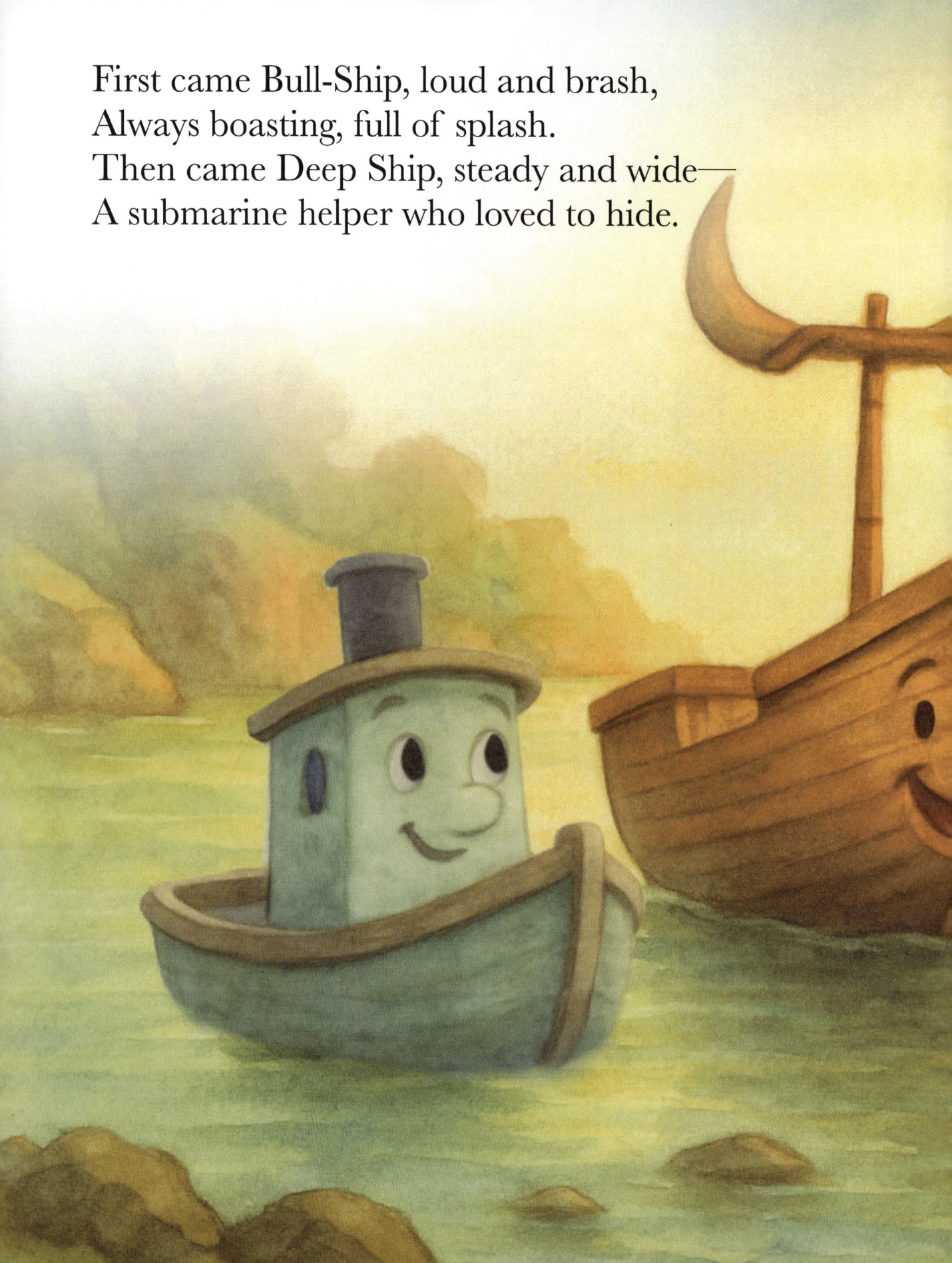

First came Bull-Ship, loud and brash,
Always boasting, full of splash.
Then came Deep Ship, steady and wide—
A submarine helper who loved to hide.

Next came Holy Ship, sails of gold,
Glowing bright - brave and bold.
Bertie laughed, "We're really clever!
Come on, crew— get your ship together!"

They patched old boats and fixed their frames,
Carving out masts and giving them names.
Each battered hull was mended and neat—
The bay now thumped with hammering beat.

But clouds rolled in, the sky turned grey,
The wind grew wild in Boggy Bay.
"The tide's coming fast!" cried Holy Ship,
As waves began to roll and whip.

"Deep Ship! we're in trouble!"
The waves were wild with bursts and bubbles!
Bertie bombed through the roaring sea,
And every ship moved valiantly.

Through crashing waves and thunder's crack,
They tied each rope tight round their backs.
Old ships reborn, their sails held tight,
They stood together through the night.

At dawn, the sea was calm and still,
Each ship stood proud with strength and skill.
The townsfolk cheered, "You've saved the day!
Our fleet's back home— hip hip, hooray!"

Now here we are, still in the bay,
Still the same ship— just a different day.
With nets to cast and fish to catch,
This town's new fleet cannot be matched.

Our two little ships were proud as punch,
Watching folk enjoy their lunch.
"Well done brave Elliot, you did great—
We got this town back in ship shape!"

Printed in Dunstable, United Kingdom